Dear Parent:
Your child's love of readi

D0490474

Every child learns to read in a different way and at his or her own speed. You can help your young reader improve and become more confident by encouraging his or her own interests and abilities. You can also guide your child's spiritual development by reading stories with biblical values and Bible stories, like I Can Read! books published by Zonderkidz. From books your child reads with you to the first books he or she reads alone, there are I Can Read! books for every stage of reading:

SHARED READING
Basic language, word repetition, and whimsical illustrations, ideal for sharing with your emergent reader.

BEGINNING READING
Short sentences, familiar words, and simple concepts for children eager to read on their own.

READING WITH HELP
Engaging stories, longer sentences, and language play for developing readers.

READING ALONE
Complex plots, challenging vocabulary, and high-interest topics for the independent reader.

ADVANCED READING
Short paragraphs, chapters, and exciting themes for the perfect bridge to chapter books.

I Can Read! books have introduced children to the joy of reading since 1957. Featuring award-winning authors and illustrators and a fabulous cast of beloved characters, I Can Read! books set the standard for beginning readers.

A lifetime of discovery begins with the magical words **"I Can Read!"**

Visit www.icanread.com for information on enriching your child's reading experience.
Visit www.zonderkidz.com for more Zonderkidz I Can Read! titles.

The Lord is faithful and will keep
all of his promises.
—Psalm 145:13

ZONDERKIDZ

Noah and God's Great Promise
Copyright © 2010 by Zondervan
Illustrations © 2010 by Dennis G. Jones

Requests for information should be addressed to:

Zonderkidz, 3900 *Sparks Drive SE, Grand Rapids, Michigan 49546*

Library of Congress Cataloging-in-Publication Data

Jones, Dennis.
   Noah and God's great promise / pictures by Dennis Jones.
      p.   cm.
   Summary: Retells, in illustrations and simple text, the biblical story of Noah,
from the time God told him to build an ark through God's promise never to send a
flood again.
   ISBN 978-0-310-71884-0 (softcover)
   1. Noah (Biblical figure)—Juvenile fiction. 1. Noah (Biblical figure)—Fiction.
2. Noah's ark—Fiction.] I. Title.
PZ7.J6835No 2010
[E]—dc22
                                                    2009004130

All Scripture quotations unless otherwise noted are taken from the *Holy Bible,
New International Reader's Version*®, NIrV®. Copyright © 1995, 1996, 1998 by Biblica,
Inc.® Used by permission. All rights reserved worldwide.

Any Internet addresses (websites, blogs, etc.) and telephone numbers in this book
are offered as a resource. They are not intended in any way to be or imply an en-
dorsement by Zondervan, nor does Zondervan vouch for the content of these sites
and numbers for the life of this book.

Published in association with the literary agency of Alive Communications, Inc.,
7680 Goddard Street #200, Colorado Springs, CO 80920.
www.alivecommunications.com

Zonderkidz is a trademark of Zondervan.

Editor: Mary Hassinger
Art direction: Sarah Molegraaf

Printed in China

15 16 17 18 19 /DSC/ 14 13 12 11 10 9 8

ZONDERkidz

I Can Read!™

READING
WITH HELP
2

NOAH
and God's Great Promise

pictures by Dennis G. Jones

Noah always obeyed God.

But Noah's neighbors sinned.

One day God told Noah,

"Since your neighbors always sin,

I am going to send a flood."

God told Noah to build an ark.

An ark is a very big boat.

The ark would keep Noah's family

and every kind of animal

safe from the flood.

While Noah built the ark,

his neighbors laughed at him.

Noah lived in the desert!

He didn't need a big boat.

Noah told his neighbors
all about the flood.

Everything on the earth would be
covered with water.

Noah's neighbors laughed harder.
They didn't think the flood
would happen.

Noah kept building the ark.

He followed God's plan exactly.

Noah made the ark very tall.

Then he put boards on the outside

and a roof on top.

After many years, the ark was done.

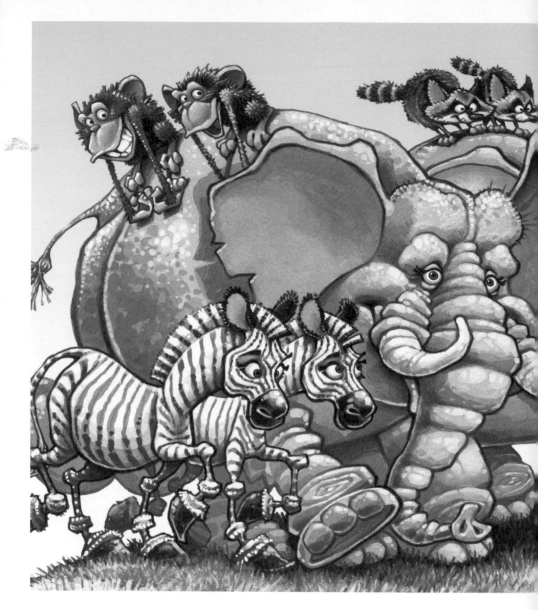

God told Noah to find

two of every kind of animal—

one male and one female.

Some animals were HUGE.

Some animals were very small.

The ark could fit them all.

More and more animals came.

Some animals ate meat,

like the lions.

Some animals ate plants,

like the rhinos.

The ark could fit them all.

Two by two,

the animals came onto the ark.

Noah stood by the door

and told them where to go.

When the last animals were inside,

God shut the door of the ark.

Everyone waited for the rain to start.

The sky got dark.

FLASH! The lightning was bright.

The flood was coming.

Pitter-patter. The raindrops fell.

And fell. And fell.

The ark began to float.

The rain made a lake that covered
the entire world.

Noah worked hard inside the ark.

He had to care for the animals.

Every day, Noah fed all the animals.

He also kept the ark clean.

Noah would check his window,

and all he saw was rain.

It rained every day for forty days.

Noah and his family were on the ark

a very long time.

Noah got tired from all the work.

After forty days on the ark,

the sun started to shine.

The water around the ark

started to go away.

Noah sent out a dove
to find dry land.

The dove brought back a branch.

The branch meant there was land.

Noah was happy.

Everyone could get off the ark soon!

When all the water was gone,

God told Noah to open the door.

The animals went to find

new homes on the dry land.

God promised to never send
a flood again.

He put a rainbow in the sky
to remind us of his promise.